CATCHMENT

THOMAS REITER

CATCHMENT *poems*

Louisiana State University Press)(*Baton Rouge*

Published by Louisiana State University Press
Manufactured in the United States of America

An LSU Press Paperback Original

Designer: Barbara Neely Bourgoyne
Typeface: ITC Galliard

Library of Congress Cataloging-in-Publication Data
Reiter, Thomas.
  Catchment : poems / Thomas Reiter
    p. cm.
  ISBN 978-0-8071-3518-1 (pbk : alk. paper)
  I. Title.
PS3568.E526C37 2009
811'.54—dc22

                              2009009894

The author offers grateful acknowledgment to the editors of the following publications, in
which the poems listed first appeared, occasionally in slightly different versions: *Appalachia*,
"This Far"; *Birmingham Poetry Review*, "Easement"; *Caribbean Review of Books*, "Rats but No
Worry"; *Caribbean Writer*, "God's Perfect Fruit," "Mocko Jumbie: Independence Square,"
"One Word"; *Cimarron Review*, "Listeners"; *Cincinnati Review*, "The Blackboard Maker
Considers the Abyss," "Inquiring Within," "A Pond at Fall Overturn"; *Crazyhorse*, "For
My Daughter on the Birth of Her Daughter," "This Time"; *Hampton-Sydney Poetry Review*,
"Bearded Fig," "The Reservoir"; *Hawaii Pacific Review*, "John from America"; *Hudson Re-
view*, "Entryways," "The Hedge Weaver," "Rehab"; *Journal of Caribbean Literatures*, "The
King of Redonda"; *Manhattan Poetry Review*, "Stones on the River"; *Ninth Letter*, "Con-
trolled Burn," "No Yard Fowl, No Sally Lightfoot Crab"; *Rockford Review*, "Prairie of the
Universe"; *Shenandoah*, "Signaling"; *Southern Humanities Review*, "Undoing"; *Southern Po-
etry Review*, "Ruth"; *Southern Review*, "The Lord's Salt," "See! I Will Not Forget You. I Have
Carved You on the Palm of My Hand"; *Tar River Poetry*, "Angelology," "How Blyden Lynch
Came Back to Perpetual Care," "Lord, Pour Water on That," "A Plantation Master's Letter to
His Sister in London," "Sugarfields Crossing"; *Willow Springs*, "Hosanna Walk."

The author also wishes to thank the McMurray-Bennett Foundation, the New Jersey State
Council on the Arts, and the National Endowment for the Arts for support during the writ-
ing of this book.

For my grandchildren

Rowan
Matthew
John

CONTENTS

CATCHMENT

SIGNALING

Broken stonework around a well,
its shaft diminished to a taproot.
A few blackened chimney bricks
in the snow. These could mark
community in the Pine Barrens,
I thought, and maybe I'd found
Ong's Hat or Aquifer or Part Way,
their post offices gone
a hundred years. In a clearing
focused by pitch pines, I watched
the topmost branches because they
wanted to show me where
I stood: their calmness buckled and
a wind-shear eddying to the ground
came up with a funnel. At first
it leaned raggedly like a candle flame
in a draft, then straightened,
now a bud vase, now a lantern
chimney. No taller than I am,
that fervor of the elements moved
lightly within the clearing.
It turned a tuft of fountain grass
inside out like an umbrella,
it gathered up the tracks
I left in the snow, made them circle
its empty center. Were we companions
on the same ground? Or there at cross-
purposes? Before I knew I would
I reached into that wheeling
self-possession, at which
my hand turned airfoil like a child's
out the window of a speeding car.

And then it came to me
what the day was building
toward. I closed my eyes
and stepped into the unrepeatable,
filling its eye. I remember
that cold torque, how in an instant
I knew it couldn't hold me yet
hold together, and how, before the snow
fell in a ring around me
I let my arms be lifted as though
signaling to someone
at Ong's Hat or Aquifer or Part Way.

SEE! I WILL NOT FORGET YOU. I HAVE CARVED YOU ON THE PALM OF MY HAND.
(Isaiah 49:15–16)

See! I will not forget you.
On the palm of my hand, July
sunlight. Where are my gardening
gloves? I took yours
down from where you hung them in May
but couldn't work my way into them,
no matter how my fingers flexed
like fish against the current. I go
bare-handed against the weeds, keeping up
disappearances because how else
will the sun be able to pull its weight
in tomatoes in this our
last garden and my first?

See! I will not forget you.
I am moving down the row easily
lifting whorled carpetweed free;
letting thumb and forefinger be enough
for lightly rooted mallows, their fruits
like wheels of cheese; unseating
the nitrogen thieves you called
fat hens, that look today
as if spring's heaped cumulus
has sown itself. And here's a plantain,
root like a vortex taking my hand
but I work myself back to the surface.
See! The ground you prepared for us
holds on. It fills my hand, this humus,
folds and parcels of garden
and none of it pouring away.

I see you adding compost and bone meal,
setting out mantis eggs against aphids.
I have carved you on the palm of my hand.

See! I will not forget you.
This garden that goes forward as I
follow, weeding, goes back
to the pellets you spilled out
on the kitchen table last March,
coins of the realm, poker chips
of peat fiber that expanded in water
into pots, each one receiving
a seed you pushed down with
your forefinger, an exclamation point.
They waited on the sunporch until
you came for them, no transplant shock. Now
they can't be told from the soil itself,
but can be said to remember you.

NO YARD FOWL, NO SALLY LIGHTFOOT CRAB

Combers breaking and the trade wind combing
palm fronds like manes this Sunday morning,
while in the sea's lulls come repentance, forgiveness
from Holiness Refuge Tabernacle on the hill.
A man is working the tide line for Tourism,
heaping into a two-wheeled cart the night's
deposit of eel grass, each leaf like a strop.
Testifying and scripture are in the wind,
with piano, banjos, drums. That joy,
and no one to shout it down as he picks up
the burden of each hymn. To the preacher's
No lions or dragons shall be there,
brothers and sisters, no earthquakes or hurricanes,
only pools of cool water, he cries *Amen.*
Hearing *God did not make man some yard fowl*
or Sally Lightfoot crab, he cries *Amen.*
A wave runs up the sand, crumbles into foam,
and in sliding back it leaves behind
a shadow, a negative of itself,
that drains from the cart's own shadow
and is lost in the mouth of the next
wave. The voices and music are over now,
done with saying how it cannot be enough,
this life, this world into which
the Four Horsemen of Revelation will ride.
Here on the sea's rostrum he pitchforks
the tide-wrack, already beginning to rot.
Over the side of his cart where it says
DEM NA WANT TO SEE A MAN STRIVE
the morning goes, reaped by the bottom currents.

REHAB

We wear harnesses like crossing guards.
In a pouch over the heart,
over stent and bypass, a black
box with leads pressed onto metal
nipples. We pedal and tread and row
while our signals are picked up
by antennas on the ceiling, X's
like the eyes cartoonists give the dead.

Angels of telemetry with vials of nitro
watch over us. We beam to their monitors
now a barn dance, now a moonwalk.
They cuff us and pump and we keep on
so tomorrow will live off today. Nurse,
we won't forget the animated
video of our cholesterol highway
where LDL, black-hatted scowling
donut holes on wheels, blocked traffic.

But with muscles like gutta-percha,
can we leave time's gurney in the dust?
By now only the dead know more about
gravity than we do. In reply, a tape
of Little Richard or Jerry Lee comes on
and we're singing, aloud or not, all
pale infarcted pedalers, rowers, treadmillers,
and our hearts are rising in the east.

THE BLACKBOARD MAKER
CONSIDERS THE ABYSS

This argument from design: a blackboard,
therefore a blackboard maker, therefore me.

Chalk grains of the day's lessons
fell to me, class clown,
because Sister Mary Perpetua had chased me
in loops through the cloakroom, the arms
of parkas waving me on while my classmates
sat with folded hands.

Slate comes from beddings of mudstone
and it shears apart in planes. I grind them
with a diamond wheel and then by hand
I swirl a grit fine as pollen.

I outdistanced her and the whole fifth grade.
Alone after the dismissal bell
I swiped everything off the blackboard.

I prepare surfaces for the world to overspread
with cursive letters, algebra, the anatomy
of a dragonfly. Whatever we do
needs to give way, and therefore I owe
my slate care, to keep it erasable.

The shells of sea animals that took form
in the abyss drifted like smoke as I
clapped erasers in the empty playground.

GOD'S PERFECT FRUIT

(St. Vincent)

A barrel for nutmegs, another for shells,
she works at a tray filled from sliding doors
at the base of a wooden hopper fed
without end from the story above
by the cracking machine's rubber mallets.

Tours begin with her station, and today
with smiles at what she chalked on the hopper,
some grains already shuddering free
and falling into the harvest:
The Lord looked at my work and smiled,
But when He looked at my pay
He bowed His head sadly and walked away.

"The floaters go into pharmaceuticals
and aircraft engine oil," she hears the guide
explain at stage #2 as he leans over
a tank, "while kernels touching bottom
are prime for your spice rack."
Twenty years of voices.
She begins saying their names to herself,
all those young men dreaming themselves
north, only these comments a constant.

She opens the doors again. Yesterday
on her way home, as she paused
to pour cinders from her shoes
on the road crossing Rabacca Dry River,
—its bed porous from ash flows—
the underground stream that can rise up
after squalls on Mt. Soufrière and sweep

lorries and school buses into the breakers
took her. Tumbling and rolling in the flash
runoff, she had a vision:
the Lord bent down to her, arms outstretched,
love pouring from that holy-picture
heart enfolded in thorns.

She found herself sitting upright
like a child in a bathtub, her legs straight out.
She'd gone nearly to the sea when the flood
fell away, soaking into the pumice
that was quickly firm underfoot again,
and no one had been swept along with her
or witnessed the journey. Nearby, her flowered
shift. It dried in the sun and wind
as she walked back the way she'd come,
unmarked, wondering how she was worthy.

She hears the guide telling
his group from a cruise ship how the nutmeg's
flesh becomes jam and syrup,
how that red filigree covering each kernel
is the seasoning mace. "Nothing wasted,"
he says at the end, "God's perfect fruit,"
and she watches her words on the hopper
tremble. Every time she opens the doors
the sound of those waters gets into
the bounty coming down from the cracking machine.

HOW BLYDEN LYNCH CAME BACK TO PERPETUAL CARE

1

What the rain and trade winds mar, he mends:
levering and jacking up the walls
of old tombs that have shifted out of true
from the time sorrow placed them there; ending
with trowel swipes feathered out.
One burial today, the last wall sealed,
and now he's back to restoration.
Pitted by salt, stricken at the seams,
doesn't stone grieve? Blyden Lynch can tell,
and only perpetual care will console.

2

Twenty years ago a pair of Americans
with matching beards like fire coral
discovered him in a rum shop and unrolled
a contract to star in a Rambo spin-off.
His Arawak, East Indian, and African blood
typecast him righteous against a WASP
drug lord corrupting Caribbean youth,
so Blyden Lynch left his apprenticeship
in tomb closing and repair
for a scrub cay in the Leewards. "Understand,
this is art we're making," the Fire Corals
bullhorned but allowed no second takes.

In posters on reggae buses the star
held his enemy in the cross hairs
of a rocket launcher, but at the premiere
he saw himself for the first time:

the audience's laughter broke like surf
against the screen. His talent?
An upper body crossed with ammo belts.
The dialogue? Banana oil. And all box office
receipts vanished from these latitudes.
*Hell be growing green vegetables before I
do such fooling again,* he vowed.

3

A squall sweeps in from beyond the reef
so he shelters his tools in a vault,
unnamed yet and open to seaward,
and climbs right in. Lightning
like the prop roots of mangroves.
Closer, he sees what his first work will be
after the rain. Chisel and wire brush,
then mortar. On the pale grayness
of a tomb beside the one he waits in,
a handsbreadth of termite tunnel runs
from the earth to a gap in the roof slab,
from this world to the next and back.

RATS BUT NO WORRY
(St. Kitts)

The Rastamen who came as Terminix
to our rental unit, who smiled No worry—
they set triggers to cheese,
they snapped off blocks of poison
the size of blackboard erasers.

Lights out and in bed now,
we remember the hole chewed through
into the pantry, that with a few
minutes more of incisor work
could have arched as smartly
as the doorway of Jerry the Mouse.

That clattering on the tiles—are rats
wearing old glue traps like snowshoes?
They don't want us to be afraid of death.
The bar of justice falls across their backs
and arteries flood their bodies,

but in their teeth the constellations
rise and set, the sea comes ashore with its wrack.

CONTROLLED BURN

One by one, wildflowers and the names
for wildflowers on this field trip
to the Konza Prairie. The teacher
gathers her second-grade class around
compass plant, rattlebox, puccoon,
and here's a calla, green flame
backed by a silver reflector
like an old lantern in Grandpa's
barn. Farther on, the footpath
enters tallgrass prairie where rangers
with tanks harnessed to their backs
poured fire from torches, turning
mats of dead grass into nutrients.
A boy crosses over unnoticed
among root mounds of bunchgrass
like scattered lumps of coal, and soon
drops to his knees. He knows by its few
unburnt feathers what this is
lying on its back across a hole
in the char: the burrowing owl
the class saw this morning on a video,
diving in slow motion with spread
wings and yellow talons, ivory ruffs
around the eyes. Touching
the owl lightly—ashes come off
on his fingertips—he imagines
the flaming sword held by that angel
in catechism this morning.
He hears his name, looks up to find
the class filing onto the bus.
On his way back he stops to kick
ashes into the air where they hang like
thunderheads, then strides right through them.

A POND AT FALL OVERTURN

Past summer's dragonflies and whirligigs,
its thunderclouds like shovelfuls

of humus, a cold wind puts its own
construction on the pond,

driving surface water down
that floated on the middle zone.

Scuds of spore from puffballs
a raccoon or hiker brushed in passing

no longer displace their weight
in birdsong on the surface film.

A waterfall within water
mists the bottom silt where nymphs

of dragonflies feed. They will ride
spring overturn along with grains

of August's algae bloom.
They will step winged from their

split skins, and all summer in flight
touch abdomens to the water like wands.

Today the cold wind unrolls its gauze
of ice. What kind of wound is this?

ONE WORD

To Alexander Hamilton out walking
in the calm center of a hurricane,
the cloud wall around St. Croix
is like the staves of a barrel.
Soon he will leave the West Indies
forever. He passes gardens where the wind
plucked out root crops by their leaves.
He passes the house, roofless now,
where his mother died in delirium.
On the table next to her he saw
a broth of herbs and a cup of her blood.

Bless this hurricane, he tells himself,
if in coming here it first
carried off from the chancery on Nevis
that birth ledger where his name was set down
18 years ago. He's read it, it says
11 January 1755, followed by
"illegitimate" in a flowing hand.

Because "obscene child" and "whore's child"
came from the mouths of priests,
his mother had him tutored by Sephardic Jews.
He remembers climbing down from a table,
a tiny Moses with blank wooden
tablets, then reciting the Commandments
in Hebrew. Alexander Hamilton laughs
aloud, declaims them as he strides
through crowds of looters—vagrants,
debtors, heretics sent here as indentured
servants by the Dutch and now carrying off
from warehouses what the hurricane hasn't.

Wind and rain again, but he finds
shelter in Fort Christiansvaern, a prison
emptied after last year's hurricane,
only one cell intact. He looks out
a window slit facing the harbor
and its waves like broadsides, point-blank.
A row of spikes lies atop the wall,
and it flashes through him, that story
his mother told about their
Huguenot ancestors. St. Bartholomew's Day,
1572, the heads of Huguenots are carried
on pikes through the streets of Paris.
He closes his eyes and can see
those heads, impaled on the prison wall,
staring at him as they have in dreams.

Four paces, and the other window
gives onto the auction grounds he crossed
coming here. He saw it was true,
what an old slave on Nevis told him,
that within the center of a hurricane
an infection in the air engenders
worms fat as a planter's fingers.

Apprenticed at 14 to import-export,
he logged in slavers from the Gold Coast.
He shaved the bodies of Ashantis,
Susoos, Mandingoes, then rubbed them with palm oil
so muscles would gleam like guilders.
He applied an herbal to remove
the yellow from the whites of their eyes.

He doesn't know how to look at chattel
in the common way of commerce, only
how to watch himself attend to them
in the way of shame. For Alexander Hamilton,
who will board a brigantine for the Colonies,
St. Croix is the odor of that oil, Nevis
a single word in a generous hand.

MOCKO JUMBIE: INDEPENDENCE SQUARE

Half hidden from us behind brimful tiered basins
of the fountain surrounded by statuary
of the nine Muses, a man climbs
onto the shoulders of another man
then steps off alone. Ah, he's a stilt walker.
His green vest is sown with ostrich
feathers, paisley pants reach to the ground.
"This a Mocko Jumbie you puzzling over," he says.

His arm sweeps over men and women gathering
for rehearsal in conical hats and checkered gowns
from the time the governor brought to St. Kitts
a troupe of jesters, and slaves mimicked them.
"Carnival tomorrow, so while the Ministry of Tourism
parades merchants' logos through Basseterre
Mocko Jumbie and clowns be pantomiming
in this square. We bring back secret revels
of ancestors in bondage spoofing the Great House."

He pauses and the falling water fills
his silence. Looking past us to the churchyard
wall that opens onto Independence Square, he says,
"You visit Massa there? His fine rose marble?
John Whitby, Master of Appleton Plantation.
b. 1750 London, d. 1803 This Bless'd Isle."
He draws a mask from inside his vest.
White skin, yellow hair. So John Whitby
pitches and wobbles trying to keep up
as the clowns cavort and play imaginary
banjos, conch shell trumpets, tambourines—
music louder than scripture and whip.

Keeping pace around the square, we watch them
now tossing wooden cane knives into the air,
spinning once and catching them,
now grinning and shivering as they rub
and hand around a mango someone then slips
into Mocko Jumbie's codpiece as he prays.

At the end all return to the fountain. Kneeling,
the clowns lift their arms above their heads,
wrists together, and a choral lament
silences the falling water. Then silence.
Mocko Jumbie takes off his mask, shoulders
his stilts. Joining the others as they leave
for Uncle Tweedy's Rum Shop, he turns
and says, "Tomorrow Babylon fill the streets
with calypso contests and hip-hop soca jamming."
Then he grins, "I wish a duppy put salt
in politicians' coffee, bones in their rice."

WINDOW SEAT

A stream of blue glass and then
something fluttering against my cheek
in the school bus: a doe's
beautiful, cartoon eyelashes. The sun
flashed along her flank as she disappeared.
Deer crossing over from fields
where builders were moving heaven and earth
fed on arbor vitae in backyards,
and nurseries stocked coyote urine.
My parents brought me home with five
stitches in my cheek and a glass
pellet the size of a pencil eraser.
The doctor let it fall from his forceps
into my hand. Next morning,
catechism and spelling and word problems
crossed the blackboard to recess
and my bragging how I hadn't cried.
I passed around what had wounded me
and lifted a corner of the bandage.
Glass and blood and the ambulance,
yes, but I told no one about
what still keeps putting me back
in the window seat so many years later:
something more than blood surfacing
to meet that gentleness,
that secret trembling against my cheek.

THIS FAR

Lying on the current's bias,
a windfall limb is covered in
driftage because every leaf
has lost its own tree. And here's
a pool, clearinghouse for
darkness and light, for cirrus
like shavings from a carpenter's plane.
Swallows start from their nests
in the bank below me, and
I see now that the opposite
bank, undercut by runoff,
has opened into itself. I cross
from stone to stone as whirligigs
run circles around me. I crouch
at the entrance to the cave
and find the roots of wildflowers
coming through the roof.
Lobelias, mallows, columbines
I have followed the stream this far
simply to stand among—
they're scud from thunderclouds,
they're knobs and knots and star-
bursts. It's all one story, then,
roots at eye level
or the earth whole and flowering,
and the creek's calling is to tell that story.

A PLANTATION MASTER'S LETTER TO HIS SISTER IN LONDON

(Barbados, 1795)

The Land of Looking Back is what my slaves
attendant upon the Great House call
this island, and do you know that in their
African language there is no future tense?
Therefore my place in their lives.
They are unworthy to work the earth
God gave us to flourish for the master's table.
In my garden today I found the harvesters
on their knees chanting and wailing. Why?
A slave on another plantation told them
that when he reached into the soil to grasp
root crops his hands came out covered
in blood. My overseer manages the cane
slaves, but those who sustain the House
as provisioners and domestics are mine.
My curse and blessing, dear sister.

As I write this, dessert of custard apples
and Madeira waits at my elbow on mahogany
from a fourteenth-century Italian refectory,
and blue morpho butterflies go
from blossom to blossom of the immortelle
arranged in stained-glass vases, its color
the most passionate orange in any latitude.
I find such beauty aids digestion.
Tomorrow I shall welcome our governor
and chief justice to dinner. The menu?
Once again the kingdom of nature
will submit to the genius of my cooks,
a divine spark in their lower natures.

Their creations are Carib and African,
and the music is in them of the four elements,
and the chiming of eye and ear and palate:
Turtle eggs roasted in a clay pot
I treasure for its fineness of mettle and
curiosity of turning, unearthed hereabouts.
Lavender crabs in a broth of casareep.
Tamarind pulped with coconut water beading
in leaded crystal. A great regalio of beef.
Muscovy duck encrusted with sweetbreads
and pimento seeds. Manatee seasoned high
with coriander, mace, and zestful peppers.
A pudding of the shy root-crop tannia
baked with star apples in the belly of a kid.

And now the Land of Brown and Gray Repast
would end all that. I have the contents
of your package arrayed before me.
Sadly, your epistle comes entirely
absent of pleasantries and instead teeming
with hortatory notions about my soul.
The letterhead tells me you are in thrall of
The Society for the Abolition of Slavery:
Spiritual Rebirth through Good Works.
So you enclose a china medallion by
Josiah Wedgwood depicting a slave
on his knees in chains, above his head
the inscription, "Am I Not Your Brother?"
And here's a penny pamphlet—Ah,
what that is meant to cost me!—on the cover
of which is a female slave tied to a wheel
and praying for mercy as the whip comes down.

But what if she had tried to poison
her master at dinner? My neighbor's fate.
The cassava bread I love, when made from
the roots of bitter manioc rather than sweet
can kill, perhaps a kitchen slave's revenge
for the discipline I am driven to.
Some entries from my journal. (I pray
you will not swoon at these measures.)
7 March. Caught Luongo in the rainforest.
First offense, so made Lacouvo, a new purchase,
piss in the runaway's eyes and ears and mouth.
21 May. Aero, who twice lost his hoe,
I tied him to a tree in the mangrove swamp
then slathered his body with molasses.
15 July. Sterling, who sneaked off to visit
his woman, I branded his testicles.

How lofty and remote your letterhead,
the bleak absoluteness of its piety.
Yet what of the world's mysterious ways?
Do we not know the Creator by the work
of His hand inspiring the work of man's?
The gourmandizing you say befouls my soul
I call an act of devotion, dear sister,
and use it to seed the Living Word
in the base natures around me. Yesterday,
while Jevanille was pressing passion fruit
for my juice at breakfast, I pointed out
to her great edification how
the crimson passion flower is an emblem:
its three stigmas signifying the nails,
its ovary the hammer, its five stamens
the wounds, its corona the crown of thorns.

Abolition? I shall affix the Wedgwood medallion
as a knob on the elegant white cedar rod
with horse-tail bristles my body slave employs
to whisk away a bowel movement's residue.

INQUIRING WITHIN

This windsock in Kansas has a hold on air
beyond wheat farmers' hold on the land.
The runway? Wildflowers have it back.
In a stand of Queen Anne's lace, dried umbels
the color of flames in a negative,
here's a wooden sign on which some local
flourishers are making spores—
lichen as a starburst or compass rose,
as a map with roads and settlements.
It reads Crop Dusting, Inquire Within.
You see the yield: backhoes take
the topsoil off, and limestone reefs
that dulled plowshares and stunted wheat
are dressed into blocks for abutments.
These westerlies in the windsock
forgotten on its tripod bring back the first
homesteaders to fail here, they bring back
women who listened to the wind
on which pollen and seeds from distances
not yet surveyed into section lines
migrated through log-and-stone walls,
who listened through hours of mending,
of stitching seams, while prairie
driftage settled on calico and denim
and the lye-soap-reddened backs of their hands,
who listened to their own childhoods
return, cries of mothers giving birth
and grandparents dying in delirium,
women who listened to grindstones in the wind
bringing edges to definition.

HOSANNA WALK

(St. Vincent)

A local steel band's logo on her T-shirt
proclaiming *Doom* below
a rainbow, she sits on her veranda weaving
root fibers, stalks, bark strips, vines
into a model of the frigate bird,
scissor tail, long tapering wings,
while Day-Glo lettered on a volcanic
boulder by her gate says, Mrs. Annie Gumbs,
Proprietor, Hosanna Walk. Her woven
tote bags, sandals, birds, and fish
go to boutiques on cruise ships
and to hikers returning from Mt. Soufrière,
dormant now, those burnt scarps and ridges
she has never witnessed, that famous
crater lake with its island of magma.
She gathers everything she needs
from the lower slopes, among the old
paths of ash flow. And sometimes,
because runaway cane-slaves hid
in that rainforest, bones will come up
clasped in roots. What can she do
but bring them home for burial?
Yesterday at a gap in the stone
foundation her great-great-grandparents set
in 1834, the year of Emancipation,
she knelt and pushed a skull through.
She breathes along a length of memory
vine and it turns supple for framing out
the body of a frigate bird whose breast
will be the bark of starvation
apple. Its wings, threads from the runners

of compass berry. She knows
how light and darkness together
drive the roots down, the stems up,
and she thinks of birth cords, being childless.
When the trading schooner her husband built,
outbound for Martinique
forty years ago, went down in a squall,
mountains and birds and flowers and trees
gaily dyed on bolts of cloth came in
day and night on the waves,
but no boatmen. It was the time of year
frigate birds hatch in the sand,
and she witnessed the truth of the legend
that breakers will hold back
at the last moment to spare the young.
*Wrap yourself in this cargo and lie down
among us, we have something to tell you,*
she heard in a dream but awoke.
Frigate birds hovering over open water,
those pirates that dive at other birds
till they drop their catch midair—
Mrs. Annie Gumbs, proprietor, Hosanna Walk,
looks up at them from her cutting and plaiting
and marks this life a mercy.

THE HEDGE WEAVER

(Anglesey, Wales)

Walking a hedge lane into the countryside
I found a crew with blue-smoke trimmers
revving those boundary shrubs
back a year in swipes and slashes.
I hurried by, and rounding a bend
came upon silence and a man, white-haired,
crouching at a ragged hedgerow
as though waiting to be let in.

And then I saw how along the other side
of that lane fronting a stone cottage, new
growth had been interwoven, tucked into plumb,
so that across its face not yet in leaf
ran a design: waves, one after another,
swelling, breaking and forming again.

He greeted me over one shoulder.
"I'm John Paget and I don't want Public Works
here. They'd rather be dole palmers
so they take it out on the hedges.
How's a story to be told after they go by?"
The ones they were being unmindful of
were yew, he told me, the limber stock
that gave Owen Glendower his longbow.

"I leave nothing to tempt a trimmer," he added.
"The facing? Different each time.
I undo the year before, prune, start again."
He pointed to the opposite hedgerow's
wickerwork: the high seas off Holyhead, where
as a young man he worked a trawler's nets.

Here in the shrub in progress, oxbows
and meanders of the River Wye
he fished as a boy. And above them
what looked like a row of wishbones,
points up. "Hazel wood's renowned for dowsing,"
he said, "forks waiting for when I hire out."
The green wood will dive after water
and mineral seams both, so the diviner's
gift is in telling one tremor from another.

I watched him braiding new shoots
into a circle of Easter palm,
into Norman stonework bordering
the baptismal font in Cardiff Cathedral
where, on furlough in 1943,
he attended his son's christening.
"And all the while," John Paget said,
"I wept and prayed for my lost mates."
Summonings and craft. He unlocked the root hoard.

STONES ON THE RIVER

All winter, letters from home
have held demolition clippings.
I set them in line but begin
with the whole length of the bridge
off its pilings, crowds gone
to cruise the new causeway,
while barge and crane maneuver
so pilots will find the Mississippi
clear for commerce when the ice is out.
Next, detonation clouds
hanging where the ironwork was
of that famous dog-leg center span—
resurrecting the town joke about
how construction halted work on WPA
public sculpture and post office murals
in two counties, capped
by some wag's letter to the editor
explaining how men in bad times see
a bridge as something larger
than themselves. Though it took
my brother ridden to the bottom
by a steel grid length of roadway
to finish the crossing in silence.
The last: a photo of plastic charges
patched along the center beams, a few
early watchers on high bluffs,
but from one approach to the other
the span in place, ice unbroken
the whole way to winter afternoons
when, coming home from school,
I climbed out on a jetty

for stones there and sailed them
with everything I had. Then took the bridge
to the other side and back
for the long look the river gave me.

THE RESERVOIR

Water for Kingstown leaves the light
behind on this rainforest lake
then picks it up again far below,
pouring into holding tanks.
Here a boy, ten, climbs after school
onto one of the steel cradles
the pipeline is strapped to, then throws
a leg over like mounting a horse.
Regulation Oxfords in his backpack,
he loves to balance in the trade
winds that sweep up from the sea
and comb the crowns of trees on the slope
above him so the mountain is like
a tall wave about to break. Walking
heel to toe or straddling the pipe
and sliding, he's going home.
He picks an overhanging mahogany pod,
crouches and taps out secret code.
He lies on his back and does vocabulary
for the next day. On a flat curve
beside a banana grove he stops again,
listening. Today the water sounds like
laughter and chatter in the rum shop
when he delivers the island's
free weekly *Buyer's Guide*.
On the wall above the urinal there's
a sheet of paper under glass, headed
"Guidebook for St. Vincent, 1900."
That was a hundred years ago.
Big letters fill the frame:
"Every Englishman in the West Indies
personifies His Majesty the King

and must not fail to utter commands
in an imperious tone. Shout
if need be. God is your authority."
When the water's low he takes out sticks
and works the pipe like a steel drum
at Carnival. He parts
vines hanging from a gumbo limbo tree
like a beaded curtain and he's in
Raiders of the Lost Ark. Near
Kingstown now he steps carefully
over laundry drying on the pipe.
This ditch passing under the main,
is it the one his teacher said
enclosed the slave quarters of a sugar
plantation, he wonders, that gully
in which the overseer kept
colonies of deadly fer-de-lance?
The boy looks hard into brambles.
He hears someone calling his name.

PRAIRIE OF THE UNIVERSE

*At a site just west of Chicago, a native tallgrass prairie is being
recreated on 600 acres of farmland within the Main Ring of
Fermilab, the world's largest proton synchroton.*
NEWS ITEM

When it comes to atoms, language can be used only as in poetry.
NIELS BOHR

That man in the distance
could be a sodbuster pacing off
his claim, at every third stride
jabbing a stake into the ground
to align furrows, except that when he
pauses and dips his shoulder
a thin stream, orange in the sunlight,
pours from a torch. Char
of corn stubble, then the prairie's
originals, seeded, coming back
while our famous particle accelerator
links the quark and the cosmos.
Beams of protons bending in the fields
of magnets circle the buried
chamber in counterflows
that collide and give rise to particles
of the moment of creation,
the curves and swirls
of the elementary: bosons, anti-
baryons, and the uncharged
neutrinos that could pass through the Earth
without touching an atom. Fire
sweeps by an abandoned burial plot
furrows flowed past for a hundred years,
that today a cutter and rake

looped a fire lane around. The stones
of homesteaders, loosened
from an outcropping, say
Henry Crawford, His Wife, Infant Son,
1877—the winter of diphtheria.
Around them, wildflowers and grasses,
panicles, spikes, umbels, every
inflorescence of prairie, their seeds
hand-gathered to be broadcast
where Henry Crawford tamped an axhead
into raw sod and dropped
the seed corn in, lightning
briary on the horizon. The proton ring
brightens with new debris
that may explain to us this universe
in which a homesteader lost between
the land office and his claim
found the family in their sod house.
He knelt on ground the plow had never broken
and began carving on the stones.

LORD, POUR WATER ON THAT

The taxi van lettered *Lord, Pour Water on That*
across its windshield pulls up in the cloud
forest, headlights soaking into blotter air,
and Mr. Bradford Lee steps down,
who for thirty years has harvested cinnamon

in the litmus blue mist of sunup
when freshly torn hardwood drips essential
oil. He rolls up bark like cigars—
chew one and there's a heat and sweetness
to surprise you. His Carib grandmother

taught him the secret of the cecropia bush
that grows here in the cinnamon's shadow,
so tomorrow in the village of Folly's Gap
where the Wag River enters the sea
he'll wrap the morning's catch in those leaves.

They instill smokiness into reef dwellers
gutted and rubbed with salt and curing
for sale on his galvanized tin roof.
This filigree vine, a helix on the trunk,
he pulls it down and holds it against

his skin a moment. Four hundred years ago,
a missionary who baptized Caribs
to die in the gold mines of Hispaniola
fled his calling for a cave in the forest
and from these fibers wove a hairshirt.

The taxi van has come back. Its passenger
door slides open that reads in Day-Glo:

Jimmy's Intensified Inn. No Loafers.
Pimps and Prostitutes—Read This and Run.
Mr. Bradford Lee, cinnamon and fish,

finishes picking what he calls the X-ray
fern, heavy with spores on the underside,
because tomorrow children will be waiting.
Pressed to the backs of their hands, a frond
imparts a chalky pattern, like bones.

JOHN FROM AMERICA

(Spoken by a high chief of the Cargo Cult, Tanna Island, Vanuatu)

1

Someday the white ships magical with cargo
will anchor at Tanna, on their broad decks
our ancestors bringing every blessing:
radios, refrigerators, Jeeps,
medicines to make us live forever,
changing old skin to new. I saw this
in a vision, though I did not fast and pray
to be singled out. A wise man named John
prophesied to me, Nampus, from the black
volcanic stone tall as a man
on the beach below this cliff. When I
awoke and knocked on that very stone
it answered "Yes," then instructed me
to remember the fathers of Tanna.

When villagers heard my vision they hurled
money and clothing from trading posts
into the sea, they buried census books
and burned their copra. To purify the children
they tore down mission schools.
They celebrated the dead and did not
weaken though the police arrested me.
That was fifty years ago, and still
I gather my council for our sea vigil,
all of us elders now. We tell stories
in which ancestors live and die,
those warriors, pearl divers, hunters—
honored so Tanna will be worthy of them.

2

The government released me after one month
when war drew close. Recruiting schooners
took young men of Tanna to Espiritu Santo
to work for Americans, unloading cargo,
and when they returned describing wonders
I knew the man named John in my vision
was John from America. My brother came back
wearing a jacket with a red cross
that John had given him, a sign that we
should set up crosses on every cliff.

Soon an American officer came
to tell us lies, that there was no messiah
named John, that no white ships would sail in
with ancestors and magical cargo.
He spoke against me, standing in the surf,
then turned his tommy gun
on a cross carved in a nearby tree.
Why should I stop believing
when I witnessed how the shadow of the black stone
drove him back into the sea?

3

Now the Tannese faith is all slash and burn,
they work on new plantations for goods
brought in from the Capital.
They deny the souls they come down from.
Smiling to one another, they ask
what the stone has been telling us,
and do we still hear the rattling of anchor chains

when Mount Tukosmeru shakes the island?
These unworthy ones who
hold back the Cargo far over the horizon,
why can't they let themselves pass
into the lives of the fathers
of Tanna? Instead, they turn away
from King Namaki, who saw Captain James Cook
standing in the surf holding a green branch,
so gave over his spear and broke off
a palm frond for that meeting of voyagers.

Patience, the black stone says to me,
and I think sometimes that our remembering
is enough, and changes old skin to new.
We build watch fires, settle ourselves
under a banyan tree slashed with a red cross,
and looking out beyond the reef
one of us begins a story.

THE LORD'S SALT

Rooted in a roadside ditch on St. Kitts
among acacias' black thorns
and leaves like skeletons of fish,
a morning glory has you
pull over and leap across the cut.
Pale blue in the early light,
each petal's notched like a hoof
where the vine, uncoiling from darkness
that can't get enough of it, curves up
over the hollow's edge. From here
the runner goes straight as a laser
toward the Great Salt Pond,
crossing waste ground where bones
can appear underfoot. The Middle Passage:
chattels piped seawater to this
salina with bilge pumps, and as the pond
ripened they raked the margin's
deepening yield, amassing dunes
for the holds of herring fleets. Escape?
The master would force a runaway
to shit into the mouth of another
then hold the jaws closed. Now
the basin fills only from storm surges.
At intervals as you follow the stem
new leaves like butterfly wings
tremble in the trade winds, their burden
to colonize. A step or two
beyond the nub of morning glory
here's a thicket of spine bushes.
At its center a tomb, a flat
marble slab raised on coral walls,
on which the salt wind has left only
Master of the Lord's Salt.

You climb down to the water, and a heron
wading for brine shrimp lifts off.
Here's a bottle but no message
to leap back with across the ditch.
The boulder standing beside you
wears a monk's tonsure of salt.

EASEMENT

Between the interstate and the unbounded
acreage of hybrid wheat, a narrow
trace of Nebraska prairie.
In a month or two, snowfall, so
the hollow stump of a cottonwood
that shaded a homesteader's sod walls
will draw a deep breath again.
Leaves of the compass plant
are deeply lobed and aligned north-south,

and the young wife from Ohio
came to love what escaped
the plow—wildflowers, their
fastness among outcroppings.
Seeds of the downy love-knot
with their gray streamers reminded her
of smoke on the wind, and when
she bent to a stalk of vervain it was like
lighting one candle with another.

She learned the ways of this place.
Mowing clumps of cord grass
to twist and knot them for fuel,
if she came upon a bush of ground cherries
she would cup a lanternlike husk
in her hands and breathe on it
to awaken the yellow seed, its power
against unfruitfulness. She knew
to get that flame in the ground and go on.

ENTRYWAYS

Good sun and drainage, so we'll turn
the soil and give it blood meal, then work
our Tom Thumb Carrot Seed Dispenser,
an inoculator's tube and plunger.
And in time install a half-pint
of ladybugs, the garden's SWAT team.

We picture carrots true as a plumb bob.
This is land my great-grandparents
Joseph and Joanna Mueller
homesteaded in 1880, that passed
unoccupied from father to son
after the Great Tornado of 1912

made staircases of the stone walls
and took Joseph and Joanna. Thickets,
a climax grove, and now we've come
to live here. We have a picture of them,
dotted swiss and denim holding hands
at the door, its hinges catching the sun.

And a pitchfork, almost out of the frame.
To clear a place for the garden
while our house goes up, local stone
for the walls and at each corner
a block that Joseph dressed, we start
with the weeds, with chicory, its

taproot a spike. The first one comes up
looking like what a two-year-old might draw
on an Etch-a-Sketch. In the funnel

of loosened earth we see a grub,
a millipede, and—what is this?—
a strap hinge, brass, on a fragment of wood.

We trowel and find more root deflectors:
a deadbolt and another hinge.
Then a pokeweed's grapnel roots
bring up the doorknob. We imagine
that door angling into the ground
and a wave of topsoil closing over it.

In their standstill that runs to
remembrance, these work up a story
in which we appear, *dei ex machina,*
a hundred years after carpentry began
turning to humus. We'll have a garden
as a way of answering the door.

THE KING OF REDONDA

You know the kind of day the counterman Fate
doesn't put his thumb in your soup?
One of those found me in residence
in the Windwards. Columbus named this
tiny island Santa Maria la Redonda,
and rotund she is, a volcanic scone
wearing a pomaded wig of guano
and with cliffs that look like Christo wrapped them.

Nothing but a blazing white sea-mark
now, population me. Harvesting stopped
when veins of phosphate more pure than guano
were found under that topping. So here I am,
sole employee of Redonda Fertilizer, Inc.,
caretaker in case the mines reopen.
I fire up a donkey engine that moves
the gears in the tramway and crusher
so they won't seize up with guano. To keep
seabirds off my roof I put up poles
flying plastic pennants like a dealership.

The counterman Fate? This morning the King
of Redonda stepped ashore from a chartered ketch.
I surprised myself by hiding, watched him
wander about in noon whiteout but had to
announce myself when he began building
a cook fire out of oleander stems.
Didn't Carib Indians kill missionaries
by wafting oleander smoke into rectories?
He opened a bottle of VSOP and we talked.

The first of Redonda's crowned heads to visit,
he was Phillipe V, and won the throne

playing darts in a London pub with the great-great-
grandson of the seaman on a guano ship
who claimed this dependency of Antigua
as his mock-heroic kingdom, bestowing
knighthoods and High Church sinecures
by the pint. What does it mean, I asked,
to have one subject only, and he a low-residency
MFA recruited in an Antiguan tiki bar
—this place a knuckle on the horizon—
because the tenure market's as tight
as every sphincter on Redonda is loose?

You deal with it by abdicating, he laughed,
scrawling on a Post-it that I was henceforth
King Phillipe VI. He planted the royal colors
in a guano bank, olive and blue stripes
torn from his late queen's bloomers, then sailed off,
a chartered accountant on holiday—but not
before calling out that he couldn't promise
he'd remember and not crown someone else.

ANGELOLOGY, DOMINICA

"Dom-in-EE-ka be how we call this island,
top adventure spot in the Windwards,"
a guide meeting his day trippers said
in the courtyard of Sans Souci
mini-mall, arts and crafts alongside
the slave auction grounds now Roseau's
vegetable market. "*We* know
where we are, but mail for us come
all moshed-up with Dominican Republic
forwarding," he laughed and led the way
to his van, emptying the mall
except for me revolving a carousel
of curios but not finding my size
in a watchband of woven palm fronds.
Then, just under the piped-in reggae,
a sudden tapping, so I looked up
and found the young shopkeeper trembling
at the register. She wore
a gold blouse and madras head-tie
for her parish's feast day
of Our Lady of Lourdes, and held in her hand
the note cards she had led me to, oils
and charcoals in a naïve style
by artists from her village. Boiling Lake
and the Valley of Desolation
struck the counter edgewise tremolo.
I followed her eyes to a man standing
where the tour group had been.
Chest and arms and legs crosshatched
with scars, glitter sprinkled
in his beard and dark, bushy hair,
he thumbnail-snapped a match to flame,

moved it slowly in a tight oval
to frame his face, hair smoldering,
then held it out toward her, crying,
"Doan you know me? Bliss. Burn.
I am de Lord God's angel. He doan ahv
bizniz but wid me. I come fuh yuh."
Behind him on the street, men coming out of
Cable & Wireless smiled at that tableau
and passed. What should I do?
Center myself in someone else's
parable? Argue angelology? Then
two women gray-haired and wearing smocks
blazoned with logos for their shops
appeared, and my naïve art
fell silent. One said to me, "No,"
so I stepped back among arts and crafts.
To the shop girl behind the counter
the other said, "Come." While I tried on
hats plaited from cloudforest reeds
three women stood at the entrance
meeting signs and wonders peaceably
to answer the angel's rapture. "Speak.
Doan you know me? Bliss. Burn."
He backed away laughing
and chanting something in patois.
The oval he had drawn at arm's length
hung there like an after-image
as I came forward to pay.

SUGARFIELDS CROSSING

The crossing keeper places her fingertips
on narrow gauge to tell if
the St. Kitts Sugarfields Express #4
is coming, cane bristling from the tops
and meshwork sides of a dozen cars.
Nothing, no whistle yet, so the white
flag stays aloft on its pole socketed
to her corrugated tin sentry box
beside Airport Road. She won't sit down
as usual in tamarind shade trackside and wait
in the bucket seat salvaged from
a crop duster, where the man she replaced
drank kill-devil rum and dozed.
No breaking contact with the rail
till she makes it say donkey engine.

Yesterday she waited for her son at
the gate of Her Majesty's Prison—ten years
for peddling ganja at Club Med,
and all the while she had reported to
the same crossing. Thirty years ago
she buried his birth cord among roots
of a lignum vitae in the rainforest,
and this morning she went back and picked
a seed pod, closing the circle.

Bound for the sugar works, he'll be riding
atop the carful of stalks he cut
this first day of sucking salt wind.
Touching him with her fingertips,
the crossing keeper will know to set out
the red flag then station herself

in front of your taxi. Seeing her,
you'll break off for a moment calculating
if what you're taking home goes beyond
the duty-free allowance. She'll bring
this world to a halt—her son is passing.

FOR MY DAUGHTER ON THE BIRTH
OF HER DAUGHTER

After school you lifted out the bird's nest
you had settled into Grandma's hatbox
and carried on the bus for show and tell.
The day before, watching helmeted men
from Power & Light high in our sycamore,
you called me to the window for
the letter U carved in the tree's crown,
held up thumb and forefinger to match it.
Now we walked the yard to learn what blue jays
build with, you carrying the fallen nest,
its flecks of shell at the bottom,
twigs radiating from the rim like arms
of a spiral nebula. Mulberry leafstalks,
yes, and low creeping wintergreen,
and branchlets—wands, you called them—
of black walnut. On your knees and turning
the nest in your hands under a lilac bush,
its leaves spattered with white as though
whoever did the October overcast forgot
to throw a tarp over them, you told me this
you loved: on your class trip to the circus
a tiny car drove honking into the center ring
and chased the ringmaster until it
sputtered, stopped, and exploded with clowns.
He fainted so they put him in the car
and ran off carrying it like a stretcher.
You wished your pen pal had been there.
Then, as I handed you a frond of cinnamon fern
you asked what it meant that the doctors
were changing the marrow in her bones.

Oh, I remember closing my eyes. But you
didn't wait, running on ahead.
You waved me over to you with a tendril
from the arbor, completing the nest.

RUTH

As I waited upwind from Leverick's
taxi, blue smoke from the engine
coursing past a limbo dancer
painted on the van in Day-Glo,
you waved me into a warehouse
on Doumerique Plantation. Its iron
roof gave your face the sheen
of volcanic sand soaked by waves.
Grenadian RootsWoman, your T-shirt
declared as you stood pinching leaves
from their branches into a barrel
for the bay rum factory.
Flawed ones drifted to the floor.

"The crops maybe grow in gold,"
you said. Three hundred years ago
a galleon took soil from the valley
to repack its oven, and during the voyage
charcoal smelted a nugget from that earth.
The vein? Still out there somewhere.
And Leverick? Still under the engine.
You shouted out the window to give up
and call the night-soil man,
the cords in your neck like buttress roots.

No excursions came to Doumerique,
no gift shop waited by the exit.
You handed me a branch, and soon
all in one motion I could pinch off
a leaf and roll its stem
between thumb and forefinger to check
both faces for parasites,

those tainters of essential oil.
"It look so the breakdown visitor
will take my place," you laughed.

Ruth, for thirty years you danced
the Doumerique cocoa harvest dry
that had soaked for purity in stone pots,
your bare feet doing steps on trays
in the sun, sliding, pivoting
to calypso from a steel drum,
turning and burnishing the seeds
to a deep mahogany so they gave off
that bitter aroma you loved.
"Too old for such now, and that
a sad affair," you said, "so I stand
daylong on cement, no end to
dividing the good from the bad."

LISTENERS

A bass tone in the mulberry grove
along my boundary draws me deeper
into deadfall. Here's the resinous note:
a branch in the wind moves across
the top strand of barbed wire dividing
my lot from Municipal Waterworks'
wells and clarifying tanks. Bark
healing and toughening over and over
has worn the barb away, and now
the wire shines like tinsel. That tank farm
with pumps and pipelines and watchmen
used to be deep woods where a man once
built a shelter from packing crates
and a tin sign lettered *Eggs.*
Collecting ferns for a merit badge
the summer I was twelve I found him.
He sat in a deck chair smoking a cigar,
his beard stained the color of pine duff.
On a stump beside him, a shortwave
receiver rigged to a car battery.
Tuning across the bands through static
like the sound of fire in dry grass
he found Greenwich Mean Time
and the weather at the South Pole
and reports from ships at sea—all
from his antenna strung between trees.
He made a listener of me
though he never knew I was hiding there.
What could you say about a man
who whistled to the music of balalaikas
on Radio Moscow? This:
one day at recess, just to watch

her face, I told timid Sister Veronica
he offered me a dollar to touch him.
At that a new self stepped out of me,
blinking at the light, and the world no longer
came to me in signals in the deep woods.
Fathers with axes leveled the shelter
and ran him back to the rail yard.
Then put up the earliest version of this fence.

THIS TIME

I go down alone on hands and knees
in the farthest corner of our lot
as we did together this time
each year. A cedar's downward
fanning branches make a lean-to,
a holdfast of shade you chose
for lilies of the valley, planting
their crowns one early May.

I see you working bone meal
and flakes of blood into cold earth,
hear you calling this a place
where winter on the way out
lets the door hit its heels. Webs
cover the handprints I left
last week as I crawled
among slugs and breaching roots
only to find the lilies of the valley
not open yet. A mistiming.

But I sat here remembering
what you showed me so many years ago:
how veins of leaves are the last
to disappear into humus,
looking like X-rays of themselves,
and how, beyond our seeing,
microponds lie among rootlets
and animals like side-wheelers
live and die there. Today
lily blossoms are pealing their fragrance
as I enter. Though they go forward
I follow them back. Oh,

I remember another name
you taught me for this flower—
St. Leonard's vesper, for the way
it sprang up where he fell
fighting a dragon
outside a monastery at evensong,
and so its love of shade.

BEARDED FIG

In a fork of Antillean cedar
or the crown of a mountain palm, any
catchment for soil gathered by the trade
winds from other islands, from Africa—

the seed of a bearded fig's
a colonist in the canopy and stays
within itself for a hundred years'
journey to the ground. Its flowers

radiant as breastplates, leaves
like quills in an inkwell for entries
in the ledgers of the New World,
like rooster tails from Jet Skis.

Its roots, thin as the horizon, spill
over the rim of the allotment.
What tree could stand against roots
that harvest the dawn mist?

They thicken decade by decade.
They girdle the trunk. And unless
an islander with a machete draws
the aerials' sap to caulk his boat,

they spiral into a sheathe and reach
the forest floor. The host rots away,
feeding the claimant that holds it
tight as coins wrapped at the bank.

UNDOING

Like hides tanning,
grape leaves lie stretched on the wire
grid of the arbor, a lean-to
shading our patio. Each year
after the harvest's put up
in jam jars and sealed with paraffin,
I unweave tendrils, flex
stems jointed like mantises' legs.
I take a clothesline pole
in each hand, set notches
to thick stems overhead, thrust,
and make the canopy decamp.
Vines balance a moment
as though I'm their flying buttress
then topple softly onto the lawn.
I cut them back toward roots
and drag the whole undoing
onto waste ground. I wrestle
the sprawl into a bundle
of overhand knots. Fire's
the term this day goes under:
the vines burn
with the sound of butcher paper
being crumpled up, flames
like a root system in air, ashes
for compost with the beans'
haggard pods, with melon runners,
with carrots soft as balsa—
the season's potlatch, to be
plowed under in the garden
and packed around the grapevine's
roots. So that in the end there's
nothing to do but step back.

www.ingramcontent.com/pod-product-compliance
Lightning Source LLC
Chambersburg PA
CBHW021348090426
42742CB00008B/781